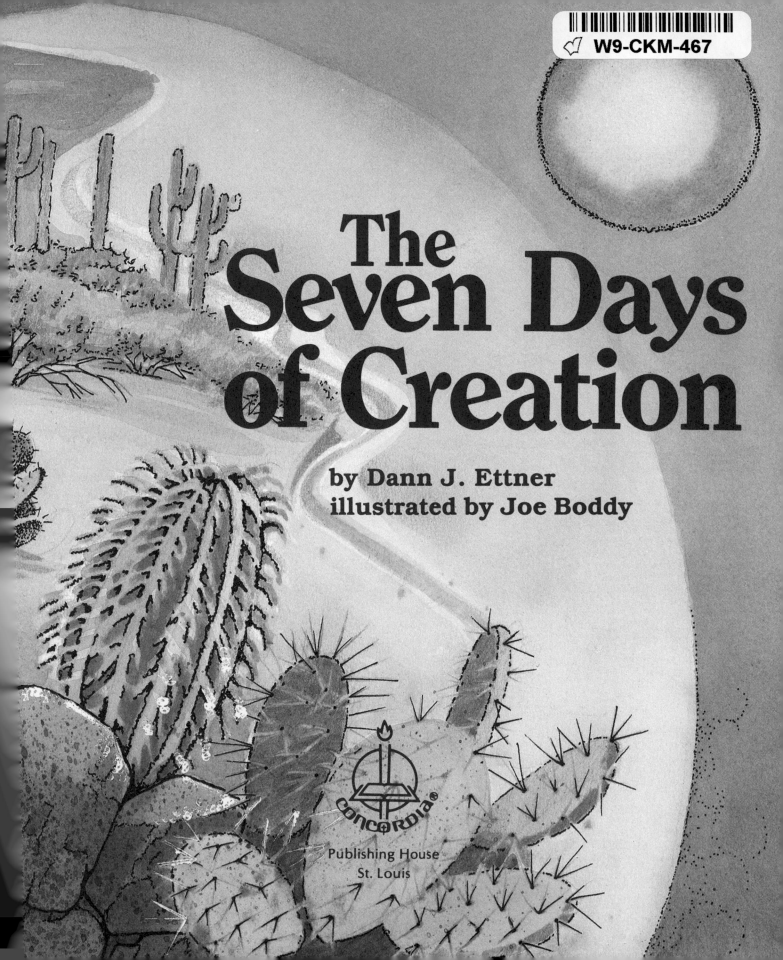

The Seven Days of Creation

by Dann J. Ettner
illustrated by Joe Boddy

CONCORDIA
Publishing House
St. Louis

Library of Congress Cataloging-in-Publication Data

Ettner, Dann J., 1957-
     The seven days of Creation.

     Summary: A book describing the work of God on each day of creation. Uses the musical score of "The Twelve Days of Christmas."
     1. Creation—Juvenile literature. 2. Bible stories, English—O.T. Genesis. [1. Creation. 2. Bible stories—O.T. Genesis] I. Boddy, Joe, ill. II. Title.
BS651.E83 1986   222′.1109505   85-17407
ISBN 0-570-04146-5

1 2 3 4 5 6 7 8 9 10   95 94 93 92 91 90 89 88 87 86

THE BEGINNING

In the beginning God created the heavens and the earth. . . .

And God said, "Let there be light"; and there was light. And God saw that the light was good; and God separated the light from the darkness. God called the light Day, and the darkness He called Night. And there was evening and there was morning, one day.

And God said, "Let there be [an expanse] in the midst of the waters, and let it separate the waters from the waters." And God made the [expanse] and separated the waters which were under the [expanse] from the waters which were above the [expanse]. And it was so. And God called the [expanse Sky]. And there was evening and there was morning, a second day.

And God said, "Let the waters under the [sky] be gathered together into one place, and let the dry land appear." And it was so. God called the dry land Earth, and the waters that were gathered He called Seas. And God saw that it was good.

And God said, "Let the earth put forth vegetation, plants yielding seed, and fruit trees bearing fruit in which is their seed, each according to its kind, upon the earth." And it was so. . . . And God saw that it was good. And there was evening and there was morning, a third day.

And God said, "Let there be lights in the [expanse of the sky] to separate the day from the night; . . ." And it was so. And God made the two great lights, the greater light to rule the day, and the lesser light to rule the night; He made the stars also. . . . And God saw that it was good. And there was evening and there was morning, a fourth day.

And God said, "Let the waters bring forth swarms of living creatures, and let birds fly above the earth across the [expanse of the sky]." So God created the great sea [creatures] and every living creature that moves, with which the waters swarm, . . . And God saw that it was good. . . . And there was evening and there was morning, a fifth day.

And God said, "Let the earth bring forth living creatures according to their kinds: cattle and creeping things and beasts of the earth according to their kinds." And it was so. . . . And God saw that it was good.

Then God said. "Let us make man in our image, after our likeness; and let them [rule] over the fish of the sea, and over the birds of the air, and over the cattle, and over all the earth, and over every creeping thing."

So God created man in His own image, in the image of God He created him; male and female He created them. . . .

And God saw everything that He had made, and behold, it was very good. And there was evening and there was morning, a sixth day. . . .

And on the seventh day God finished His work which He had done, and He rested on the seventh day from all His work.

—Genesis 1:1–2:2

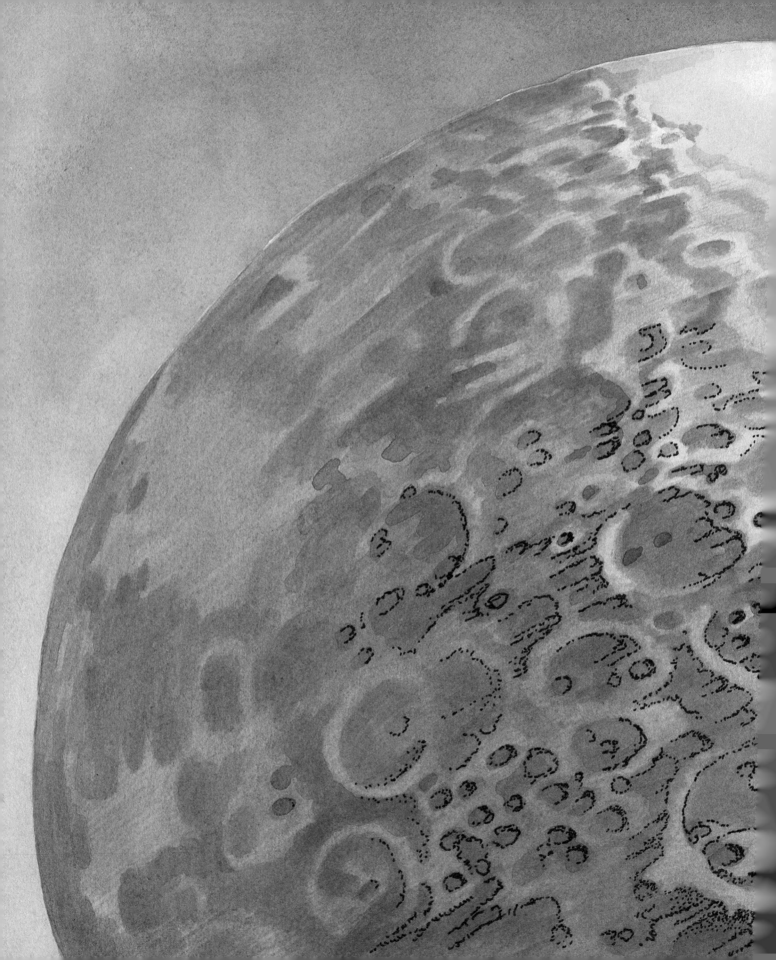

On the first day of creation
my dear Lord gave to me:
  A night and a day to praise God.

On the second day of creation my dear Lord gave to me:
  The clear, blue sky;

And a night and a day to praise God.

On the third day of creation my dear Lord gave to me:
    Oceans and mountains;

The clear, blue sky;
And a night and a day
to praise God.

On the fourth day of creation my dear Lord gave to me:
A bright shining sun;

Oceans and mountains;
The clear, blue sky;
And a night and a day to praise God.

On the fifth day of creation my dear Lord gave to me:
Little birds and fish;

A bright shining sun;
Oceans and mountains;
The clear, blue sky;
And a night and a day
  to praise God.

On the sixth day of creation
my dear Lord gave to me:
    Animals and me;

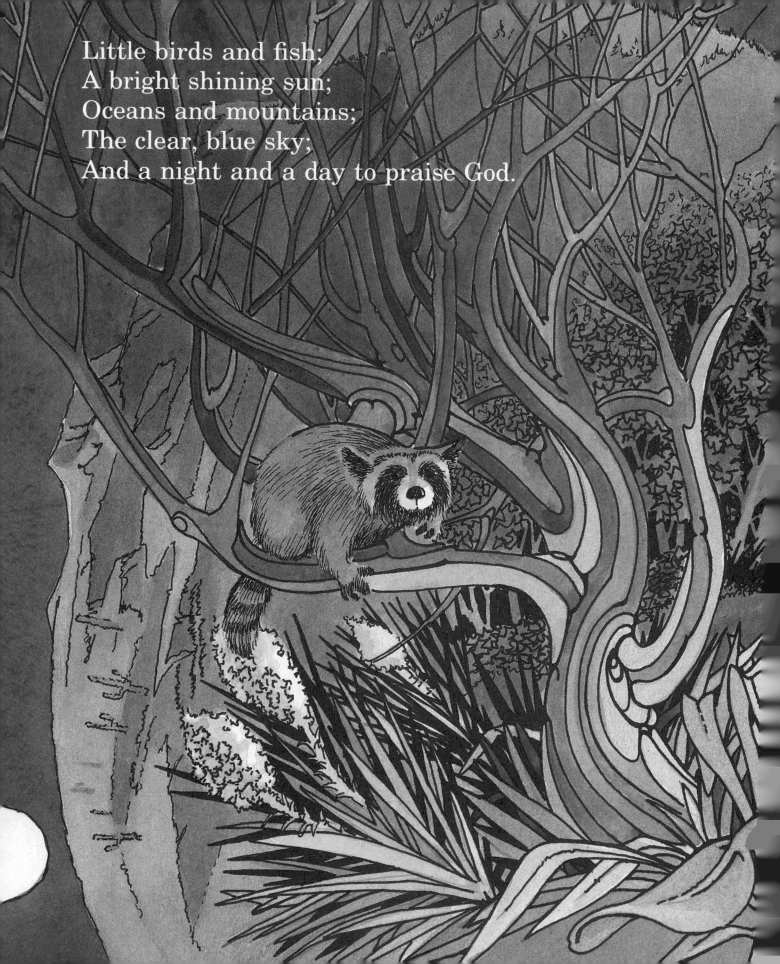

Little birds and fish;
A bright shining sun;
Oceans and mountains;
The clear, blue sky;
And a night and a day to praise God.

On the seventh day of creation
my dear Lord gave to me:
    A day of rest;

Animals and me;
Little birds and fish;
A bright shining sun;
Oceans and mountains;
The clear, blue sky;
And a night and a day to praise God.

The Seven Days of Creation

Dann J. Ettner

Traditional carol

Verse 1

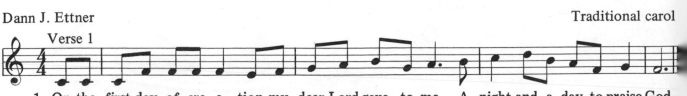

1. On the first day of cre-a-tion my dear Lord gave to me A night and a day to praise God.

Verses 2-4

2. On the sec-ond day of cre-a-tion my dear Lord gave to me
3. On the third__ day of cre-a-tion my dear Lord gave to me
4. On the fourth__ day of cre-a-tion my dear Lord gave to me A

2

3,4

The clear blue sky, And a night and a day to praise God. (3) O-ceans and moun-tains,
(4) bright shin-ing sun,__ [repeat 2]
[repeat 3,2]

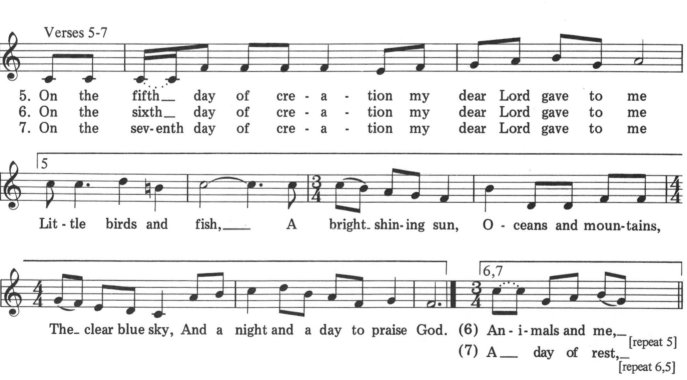

Verses 5-7

5. On the fifth__ day of cre-a-tion my dear Lord gave to me
6. On the sixth__ day of cre-a-tion my dear Lord gave to me
7. On the sev-enth day of cre-a-tion my dear Lord gave to me

5

Lit-tle birds and fish,__ A bright__ shin-ing sun, O-ceans and moun-tains,

6,7

The__ clear blue sky, And a night and a day to praise God. (6) An-i-mals and me,__
(7) A __ day of rest,__ [repeat 5]
[repeat 6,5]

A NOTE TO PARENTS

The Seven Days of Creation provides children with an enjoyable way to learn what God did during each of the first seven days of the world. The fun repetition of the song (sung to the melody of "The Twelve Days of Christmas") effectively reinforces the content of God's words in His Word. Selections from Gen. 1:1–2:2 are printed in the front of the book. You may wish to substitute from a translation familiar to your child, or from a "children's Bible."

To extend your child's learning, look at the illustrations for each day of creation. Discuss the items shown. Ask what other things were created on that day. For example, for the third day, your child might include rivers, rocks, and the plants he or she knows (including vegetables).

As you discuss day 6, talk about God's special creation of Adam and Eve. Refer to the details in Genesis 2:7. Discuss also God's plan for families. Such early discussions help lay the foundation for a lifelong Christian commitment to marriage.

When discussing the seventh day, talk about why we call Sunday "the Lord's Day" and about ways to honor it. This includes Sunday school and worship—but there can be more. Some parents use the day to focus on the family through group events. Others use it as a day of quiet meditation (if the children are old enough to hold back their energies by themselves).

May the Lord bless your time together as you grow under God's Word.

The Editor